ALLAN AHLBERG

Chicken, Chips and Peas

Illustrated by
ANDRÉ AMSTUTZ

VIKING • PUFFIN

PUFFIN
Published by the Penguin Group: London, New York, Australia, Canada, India, New Zealand and South Africa
Penguin Books Ltd, Registered Offices: 80 Strand, London WC2R 0RL, England

First published by Viking 1999
1 3 5 7 9 10 8 6 4 2
Published in Puffin Books 1999
13 15 17 19 20 18 16 14

Text copyright © Allan Ahlberg, 1999
Illustrations copyright © André Amstutz, 1999
All rights reserved

The moral right of the author and illustrator has been asserted

Printed in Italy by Printer Trento Srl

A CIP catalogue record for this book is available from the British Library
ISBN 0–670–87991–6 Hardback
ISBN 0–140–56397–0 Paperback

Fast Fox wakes up.
He wants his supper –
chicken, chips and peas.

Mother Hen wakes up.
Her chickens want their supper –
corn, corn . . . and corn.

Slow Dog wakes up . . .
and goes to sleep again.

Fast Fox looks in his freezer.
Chips – yes!
Peas – yes!
But *no* chicken.

Mother Hen looks in her cupboard.
The chickens look too.
But *no* corn.

Slow Dog looks . . . nowhere.

The chickens go out to find some corn.

Fast Fox goes out to find some chickens.

Mother Hen answers the phone.
Slow Dog . . . yawns.

The chickens look here and there.
They find a bat.
They find a ball.
They find a toy truck
with a teddy in it.

But *no* corn.

Fast Fox looks here and there.
He finds a beehive.
He finds a bee!

He finds a paddling pool
with a toy duck in it.
But *no* chickens.

Then . . .
the chickens find the corn
and Fast Fox finds . . .

T H

E M !

Fast Fox chases the chickens.

Mother Hen chases Fast Fox.

Slow Dog chases . . . nobody.

Fast Fox *catches* the chickens,
and Mother Hen too.
He puts them in his supper sack
and hurries home.

... falls on Fast Fox
and knocks him flat.

So the story ends.

The chickens get corn for supper and a bedtime story.

Slow Dog gets a pat on the head and a biscuit from Mother Hen.

Fast Fox gets a *lump* on the head,
a black eye
and a long walk home.

He gets his supper too.
Chips – yes!
Peas – yes!

But *no* chicken.

The End

THE FAST FOX, SLOW DOG BOOKS

If you have enjoyed this story,
why not read another?
Try

Slow Dog Falling

In *Slow Dog Falling*,
Mother Hen is on the phone,
Slow Dog is all tied up,
Fast Fox is reading his cookbook,
and *chicken* is on the menu.

Oh no!
Those poor little chickens . . .

. . . who will save them?